DESHAUN WATSON

SUPERSTAR QUARTERBACK

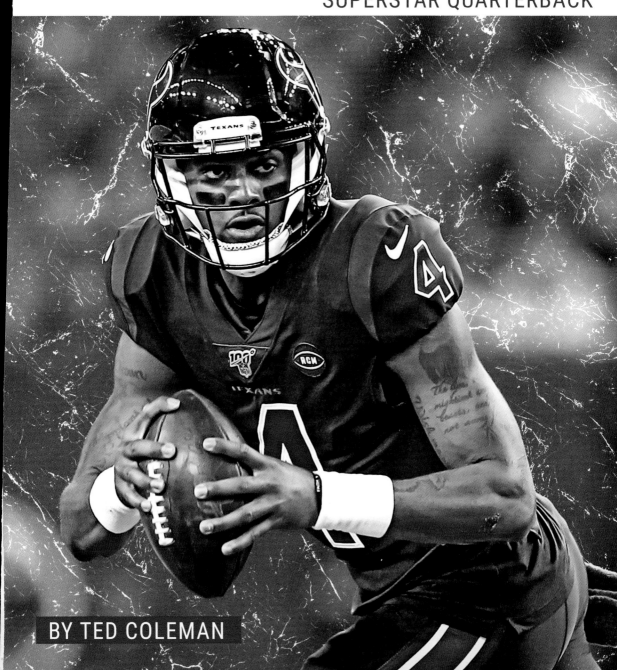

BY TED COLEMAN

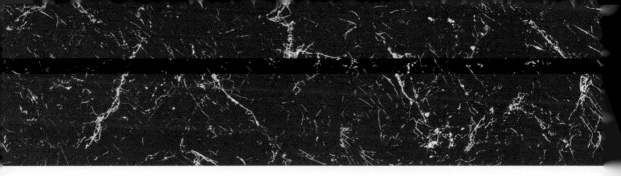

Book design by Jake Nordby
Cover design by Jake Slavik

Photographs ©: Greg Trott/AP Images, cover, 1, 23; Margaret Bowles/AP Images, 4; John Mersits/Cal Sport Media/AP Images, 7; Jason Getz/Atlanta Journal-Constitution/AP Images, 8; Bob Leverone/AP Images, 11; Tim Warner/Cal Sport Media/AP Images, 13; David J. Phillip/AP Images, 14, 19; Kirby Lee/AP Images, 17; Ryan Kang/AP Images, 20; Cooper Neill/AP Images, 25; Eric Christian Smith/AP Images, 26–27; Shutterstock Images, 27; Red Line Editorial, 29; Peter Read Miller/AP Images, 30

Press Box Books, an imprint of Press Room Editions.

Library of Congress Control Number: 2020901606

ISBN
978-1-63494-214-0 (library bound)
978-1-63494-232-4 (paperback)
978-1-63494-250-8 (epub)
978-1-63494-268-3 (hosted ebook)

Distributed by North Star Editions, Inc.
2297 Waters Drive
Mendota Heights, MN 55120
www.northstareditions.com

Printed in the United States of America
082020

About the Author
Ted Coleman is a sportswriter who lives in Louisville, Kentucky.

TABLE OF CONTENTS

1 EYE OF THE TIGER

The crowd was roaring. Alabama fans were hoping their defense could make a stop. Clemson fans were pushing their team to make a comeback. Clemson quarterback Deshaun Watson didn't hear any of it. He was focused on driving his team to victory.

Watson and the Tigers had just fallen behind Alabama 31–28 late in the College Football Playoff National Championship game in January 2017. The Tigers had the ball on their own 32-yard line. Just over

Deshaun Watson took advantage of his last chance to drive Clemson down the field.

two minutes remained in the game. Watson wanted to take the lead back for good.

He started with a 5-yard completion. Then Watson threw a 24-yard strike to advance the ball into Alabama territory. He completed three more passes as Clemson reached the Alabama 9-yard line. The Tigers took a timeout with 14 seconds left.

Watson tried a pass into the end zone, but he overthrew the receiver. Nine seconds were left. Watson then lobbed another pass into the end zone, but it fell incomplete. But a penalty on Alabama gave Clemson the ball at the 2-yard line. Only six seconds remained.

NFL STARS

Six Clemson players from the national title game were taken in the 2017 National Football League (NFL) Draft. Watson was chosen by the Houston Texans. He was one of two Clemson players taken in the first round.

Watson (4) had already begun to celebrate as Hunter Renfrow (13) caught the touchdown pass.

Watson had one last chance. He rolled to his right. Wide receiver Hunter Renfrow was open in the front of the end zone. Watson hit him with a short pass. Touchdown! Clemson won 35-31. The Tigers were national champions.

Watson finished the day with an amazing 420 passing yards and three touchdown passes. But Clemson fans were used to seeing him perform under pressure.

2 YOUNG STAR

Deshaun Watson was born in Gainesville, Georgia, on September 14, 1995. Growing up in Gainesville, about an hour northeast of Atlanta, Deshaun loved playing pickup basketball and football with his friends. His dreams of being a football player began in elementary school.

Deshaun already had the natural talent. He was named the starting quarterback of his high school team as a freshman. That was no small feat. It was the first time in

Deshaun was a four-year starter at Gainesville High School in Georgia.

more than 30 years of coaching that Gainesville High School's head coach had started a freshman.

Deshaun set state records for passing yards and touchdown passes. But he was also effective with his feet. He set records for total yards and touchdowns as well. He led Gainesville to a state title his junior season.

Some of the best college football programs in the country wanted Deshaun to play for them. He had offers from Ohio State, Alabama, Louisiana State (LSU), and more. But the first program to offer him a scholarship was Clemson. Deshaun committed to play for the Tigers.

Deshaun was confident he could win the starting job right away. It didn't happen exactly like that. Senior Cole Stoudt was the

Deshaun throws one of his six touchdown passes against North Carolina during his freshman year.

starter in Week 1. But Deshaun still got some playing time.

And Deshaun made the most of his opportunities. In a game against South Carolina State, the Tigers scored on all four of his drives, three on touchdown passes. After three games, Deshaun was named the starter. The next week, he threw six touchdown passes to beat North Carolina. But injuries slowed him down, and Stoudt regained the starting job.

There was no question Deshaun would be the starter for 2015. And he was as good as promised. The Tigers went undefeated and were ranked No. 1 at the end of the regular season. Clemson advanced to the College Football Playoff National Championship game against Alabama. Deshaun played a great game. He threw for more than 400 yards and four touchdowns. But the game was a shootout, and Clemson ran out of chances. The Crimson Tide won 45-40.

A TREASURED GIFT

Deshaun's family struggled financially during his childhood. Gainesville was not a wealthy community. The Watson family lived in housing that was provided by the government. When Deshaun was 11, his family received a home of their own through the Habitat for Humanity program. The house was furnished by Atlanta Falcons running back Warrick Dunn. Deshaun later became a ball boy for the Falcons and learned how hard NFL players work.

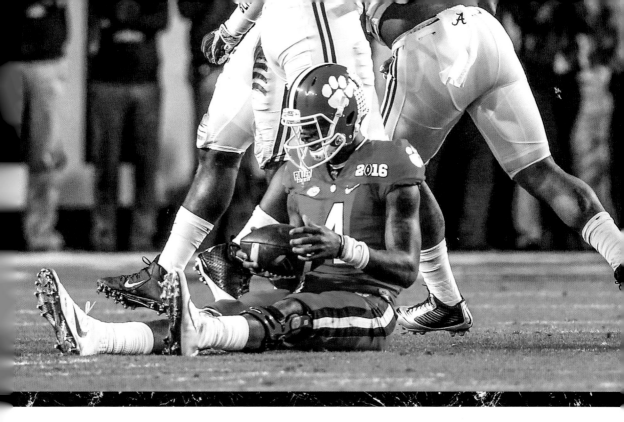

Deshaun and the Tigers came up just short against Alabama in January 2016.

The Tigers got their revenge the next year. Deshaun led Clemson to its first national title since 1981. And he was offensive Most Valuable Player (MVP) of the title game. There was no question Deshaun was one of the greatest quarterbacks in the country. The next step was to see what he could do in the NFL.

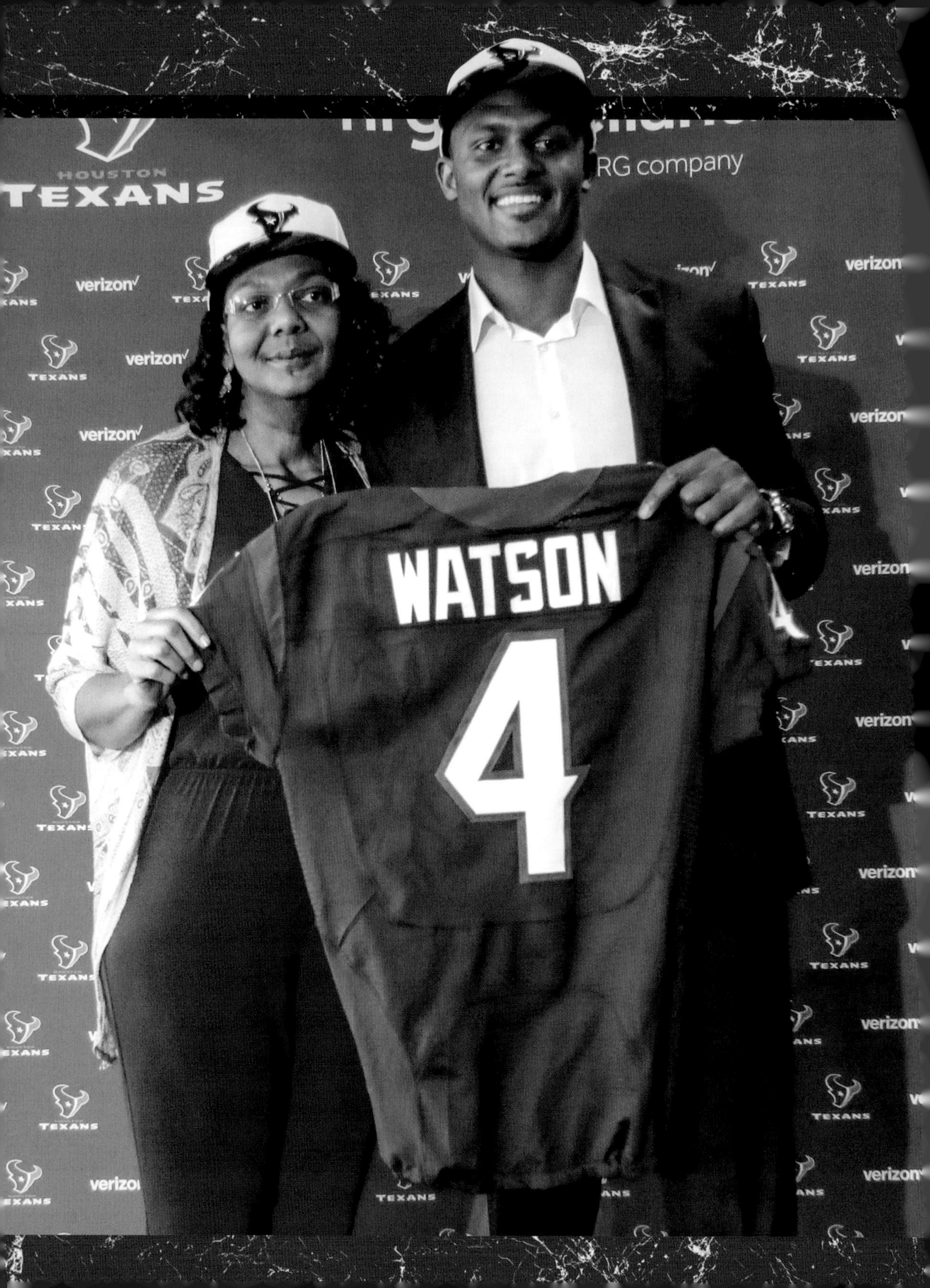
HOUSTON
TEXANS
RG company
verizon
WATSON
4

3 BECOMING TEXAN

Some experts rated Deshaun Watson the top quarterback in the 2017 NFL Draft. But Watson watched as two quarterbacks were picked ahead of him. Chicago took Mitchell Trubisky at No. 2. The Chiefs traded up to select Patrick Mahomes at No. 10.

The Houston Texans really wanted Watson. They were a playoff team in 2016 but didn't have a strong quarterback. Houston made a trade to move up and take him at No. 12.

Watson and his mother, Deann, pose for a photo after he was drafted by the Houston Texans.

Watson believed he should have been the first quarterback taken. That motivated him to prove himself with the Texans.

Watson was unable to beat out Tom Savage for the 2017 starting job. But that arrangement didn't survive the first game. After Savage was sacked six times and fumbled twice, Watson came in. He threw his first career touchdown pass in the third quarter. It was too late to save the game, but Watson became the starter the next week.

It just happened to be Watson's 22nd birthday. He was the one giving gifts as he led Houston to a 13–9 win at Cincinnati. Watson stole the show with his rushing skills. He scored the game's only touchdown on a 49-yard run in the second quarter.

Watson breaks free for a long touchdown run against the Bengals in his first career start.

The next week was a tough test against the Super Bowl champion New England Patriots. The Texans lost 36–33, but Watson threw for 301 yards and two touchdowns. His breakout game came the next week against the Tennessee Titans. He threw for four touchdowns and ran for another. The five total touchdowns tied an NFL rookie record.

The stats and records just kept coming for Watson. He threw five touchdown passes against the Kansas City Chiefs. In the month of October, Watson threw for 16 touchdowns. He was named the conference Offensive Player of the Month.

HELPING HOUSTON

Hurricane Harvey devastated Houston just before the start of the 2017 NFL season. Watson was brand new to the Houston community. But to help out, he donated his first NFL paycheck to three workers at the team cafeteria whose lives had been disrupted by the hurricane. The check was worth approximately $27,000.

But injuries again ended a promising season. Watson was practicing on November 2 when he landed awkwardly on his right leg. At first he didn't think it was serious. But tests revealed a torn ligament, the same injury he'd had in college but on his other leg. He was out for the season.

Watson had to watch the second half of his rookie season from the sidelines after injuring his right knee in practice.

The Texans were 3–4 with Watson in the lineup. But they went 1–8 the rest of the way without him. Watson finished his rookie year with 1,699 passing yards. He threw 19 touchdown passes and just eight interceptions. It was a great start. But Watson knew he had a lot more to give.

4 STANDING TALL

Watson was fully healthy for the 2018 season. But that changed quickly. He got sacked 25 times in the first six games. He suffered a broken rib and a collapsed lung. The lung injury meant Watson could not fly. He had to take a bus to Houston's seventh game. It was in Jacksonville, Florida—a 12-hour drive.

Watson overcame the long ride and his injuries to lead Houston to a 20-7 win. And the Texans kept rolling, finishing 11-5 and winning their division. Watson got to

Watson battled through more injuries but still managed to thrive in 2018.

make his first playoff start. But the offense was quiet in a 21–7 loss to the Indianapolis Colts.

The Texans and Watson put together another solid season in 2019. Again they went 11–5. Again they won their division. But fans and players alike were focused on the playoffs. Could their team take the next step? Their first chance was at home against the Buffalo Bills in the wild-card round.

Watson had played in big games before. He showed at Clemson he knew how to win them. But the Texans offense was again quiet. They trailed the Bills 16–0 in the third quarter. Then Watson started a comeback.

Watson ran for a touchdown and two-point conversion late in the third quarter. Then the Texans made a field goal. Then Watson threw for a touchdown and two-pointer late in the

Watson used his legs to get the Texans back into the game against Buffalo.

fourth quarter. Just like that, the Texans had a lead with 4:37 to go in the game.

But Buffalo made a last-gasp field goal to force overtime. The teams traded scoreless possessions. Then Watson had another chance. He drove the Texans to the Buffalo

44-yard line. They were close to field goal range. But they needed more.

Watson faced second down and six yards to go. Buffalo's defense rushed at him from both sides. Two players hit him at the same time. Amazingly, Watson shrugged off their hits and spun out of the way. He took off to his right and found running back Taiwan Jones open 10 yards away. Jones caught the pass and slipped away from the Bills defenders.

Jones took the ball all the way to Buffalo's 10-yard line. That set up a short field goal for Houston's Ka'imi Fairbairn. He nailed it, and the Texans advanced in the playoffs.

"Somebody had to be great," Watson said afterward. "Why not me?"

The next week in Kansas City, Watson threw two touchdown passes as the Texans took a

Though the season didn't end the way Texans fans wanted it to, they knew the team would be back in the playoffs again with Watson under center.

24-0 lead in the second quarter. But the Chiefs roared back for a 51-31 victory. It was a tough way to end an amazing season. But Watson had Texans fans believing that bigger things were in store.

KING COMEBACK

Watson has made a habit out of making comebacks. Through 2019 Watson had brought his team from behind in the fourth quarter eight times. That was already tied for 21st among active quarterbacks in just three seasons.

THE GREAT ESCAPE

Deshaun Watson took a beating in Houston's 2020 playoff win over Buffalo. The Bills sacked him seven times and had 12 quarterback hits. But on the play of the game, Watson stared down two charging defenders and lived to tell about it.

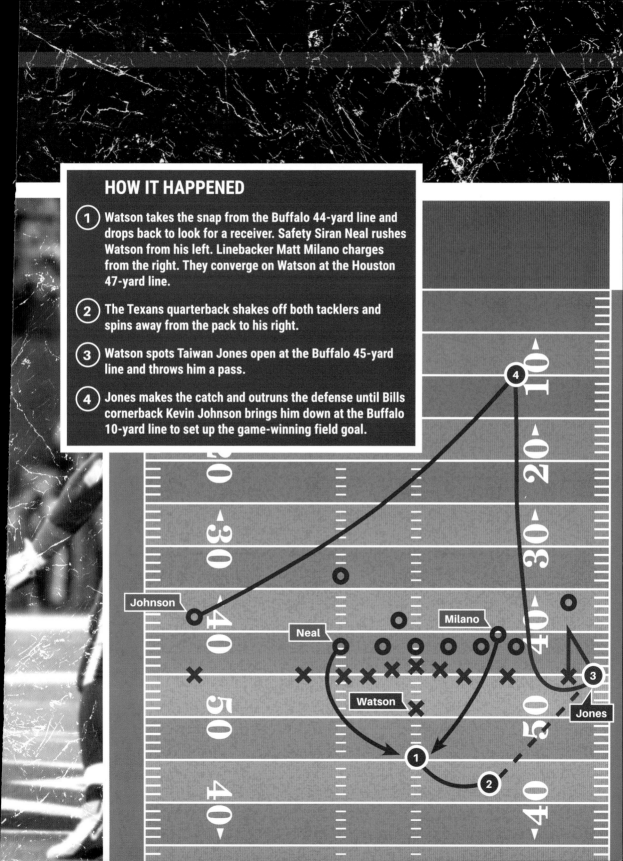

HOW IT HAPPENED

1 Watson takes the snap from the Buffalo 44-yard line and drops back to look for a receiver. Safety Siran Neal rushes Watson from his left. Linebacker Matt Milano charges from the right. They converge on Watson at the Houston 47-yard line.

2 The Texans quarterback shakes off both tacklers and spins away from the pack to his right.

3 Watson spots Taiwan Jones open at the Buffalo 45-yard line and throws him a pass.

4 Jones makes the catch and outruns the defense until Bills cornerback Kevin Johnson brings him down at the Buffalo 10-yard line to set up the game-winning field goal.

Johnson

Neal

Milano

Watson

Jones

TIMELINE

1. ## Gainesville, Georgia (September 14, 1995)
   Deshaun Watson is born.

2. ## Clemson, South Carolina (2014)
   Watson begins attending Clemson University.

3. ## Athens, Georgia (August 30, 2014)
   Watson plays in his first game for the Clemson Tigers, completing 2 of 4 passes for 59 yards and a touchdown against Georgia.

4. ## Glendale, Arizona (January 11, 2016)
   Watson throws four touchdown passes in the national championship game, but Alabama beats the Tigers 45–40.

5. ## Tampa, Florida (January 9, 2017)
   Watson leads the Tigers to their first national championship since 1981, beating Alabama 35–31.

6. ## Cincinnati, Ohio (September 14, 2017)
   Watson makes his first NFL start in a 13–9 win over the Cincinnati Bengals.

7. ## Houston, Texas (January 4, 2020)
   Watson wins his first NFL playoff game, leading a 22–19 comeback win over the Buffalo Bills.

MAP

AT-A-GLANCE

Birth date: September 14, 1995

Birthplace: Gainesville, Georgia

Position: Quarterback

Throws: Right

Height: 6 feet 2 inches

Weight: 220 pounds

Current team: Houston Texans (2017–)

Past teams: Clemson University Tigers (2014–16)

Major awards: Pro Football Writers of America (2017), NFL All-Rookie Team (2017), College Football Playoff National Champion (2016), Consensus All-American (2015)

Accurate through the 2019 NFL season and playoffs.

GLOSSARY

breakout
A notable performance early in one's career that shows promise for the future.

comeback
When a team rallies to take the lead in a game it had been losing.

draft
A system that allows teams to acquire new players coming into a league.

end zone
The end of the field where teams try to score touchdowns.

freshman
A first-year student.

fumbled
Let go of the ball, allowing it to be recovered by the other team.

ligament
A piece of tissue in the body that connects bones to other bones.

pickup
An informal game.

rookie
A first-year player.

scholarship
Money awarded to a student to pay for education expenses.

TO LEARN MORE

Books

Kaminski, Leah. *Clemson Tigers*. New York: AV2 by Weigl, 2020.

Ryan, Todd. *Houston Texans*. Minneapolis, MN: Abdo Publishing, 2020.

York, Andy. *Ultimate College Football Road Trip*. Minneapolis, MN: Abdo Publishing, 2019.

Websites

Deshaun Watson College Stats
www.sports-reference.com/cfb/players/deshaun-watson-1.html

Deshaun Watson Pro Stats
www.pro-football-reference.com/players/W/WatsDe00.htm

Houston Texans
www.houstontexans.com

INDEX